Sarah Beckwith

ALL THAT FALL

other works by the same author

★

WAITING FOR GODOT

ENDGAME

KRAPP'S LAST TAPE *and* EMBERS

HAPPY DAYS

EH JOE

PLAY

NOT I

All That Fall

A Play for Radio

by

SAMUEL BECKETT

FABER AND FABER
London & Boston

·First published in 1957
by Faber and Faber Limited
3 Queen Square London WC1
First published in this edition 1965
Reprinted 1966, 1969, 1970, 1975 and 1978
Printed in Great Britain by
Whitstable Litho Ltd Whitstable Kent
All rights reserved

© 1957 Samuel Beckett

ISBN 0 571 06336 5

CAST

MRS. ROONEY (Maddy)	a lady in her seventies
CHRISTY	a carter
MR. TYLER	a retired bill-broker
MR. SLOCUM	Clerk of the Racecourse
TOMMY	a porter
MR. BARRELL	a station-master
MISS FITT	a lady in her thirties
A FEMALE VOICE	
DOLLY	a small girl
MR. ROONEY (Dan)	husband of Mrs. Rooney, blind
JERRY	a small boy

ALL THAT FALL was commissioned by the B.B.C. and was first broadcast in the Third Programme on 13 January 1957. It was produced by Donald McWhinnie. The cast was as follows:

MRS. ROONEY	Mary O'Farrell
CHRISTY	Allan McClelland
MR. TYLER	Brian O'Higgins
MR. SLOCUM	Pat Magee
TOMMY	Jack MacGowran
MR. BARRELL	Harry Hutchinson
MISS FITT	Sheila Ward
A FEMALE VOICE	Peggy Marshall
MR. ROONEY	J. G. Devlin
JERRY	Terrance Farrell

and members of the B.B.C. Drama Repertory Company

Kenner "radio proves to be the perfect medium for B's primary concern: the relationship between words, silence and existence"

*Rural sounds. Sheep, bird, cow, cock, severally, then
together.*

Silence.

*Mrs. Rooney advances along country road towards
railway-station. Sound of her dragging feet.
Music faint from house by way. "Death and the
Maiden." The steps slow down, stop.*

MRS. ROONEY: Poor woman. All alone in that ruinous old house.

*Music louder. Silence but for music playing.
The steps resume. Music dies. Mrs. Rooney murmurs,
melody. Her murmur dies.* Schubert
*Sound of approaching cartwheels. The cart stops.
The steps slow down, stop.*

MRS. ROONEY: Is that you, Christy?

CHRISTY: It is, Ma'am.

MRS. ROONEY: I thought the hinny was familiar. How is your
poor wife?

CHRISTY: No better, Ma'am.

MRS. ROONEY: Your daughter then?

CHRISTY: No worse, Ma'am.

Silence.

MRS. ROONEY: Why do you halt? (*Pause.*) But why do I halt?

Silence.

CHRISTY: Nice day for the races, Ma'am.

MRS. ROONEY: No doubt it is. (*Pause.*) But will it hold up?
(*Pause. With emotion.*) Will it hold up?

Silence.

CHRISTY: I suppose you wouldn't——

MRS. ROONEY: Hist! (*Pause.*) Surely to goodness that cannot be
the up mail I hear already.

Silence. The hinny neighs. Silence.

7

CHRISTY: Damn the mail.

MRS. ROONEY: Oh thank God for that! I could have sworn I heard it, thundering up the track in the far distance. (*Pause.*) So hinnies whinny. Well, it is not surprising.

CHRISTY: I suppose you wouldn't be in need of a small load of dung?

MRS. ROONEY: Dung? What class of dung?

CHRISTY: Stydung.

MRS. ROONEY: Stydung . . . I like your frankness, Christy. (*Pause.*) I'll ask the master. (*Pause.*) Christy.

CHRISTY: Yes, Ma'am.

MRS. ROONEY: Do you find anything . . . bizarre about my way of speaking? (*Pause.*) I do not mean the voice. (*Pause.*) No, I mean the words. (*Pause. More to herself.*) I use none but the simplest words, I hope, and yet I sometimes find my way of speaking very . . . bizarre. (*Pause.*) Mercy! What was that?

CHRISTY: Never mind her, Ma'am, she's very fresh in herself today.
Silence.

MRS. ROONEY: Dung? What would we want with dung, at our time of life? (*Pause.*) Why are you on your feet down on the road? Why do you not climb up on the crest of your manure and let yourself be carried along? Is it that you have no head for heights?
Silence.

CHRISTY: (*to the hinny*). Yep! (*Pause. Louder.*) Yep wiyya to hell owwa that!
Silence.

MRS. ROONEY: She does not move a muscle. (*Pause.*) I too should be getting along, if I do not wish to arrive late

8

at the station. (*Pause.*) But a moment ago she neighed and pawed the ground. And now she refuses to advance. Give her a good welt on the rump. (*Sound of welt. Pause.*) Harder! (*Sound of welt. Pause.*) Well! If someone were to do that for me I should not dally. (*Pause.*) How she gazes at me to be sure, with her great moist cleg-tormented eyes! Perhaps if I were to move on, down the road, out of her field of vision . . . (*Sound of welt.*) No, no, enough! Take her by the snaffle and pull her eyes away from me. Oh this is awful! (*She moves on. Sound of her dragging feet.*) What have I done to deserve all this, what, what? (*Dragging feet.*) So long ago . . . No! No! (*Dragging feet. Quotes.*) "Sigh out a something something tale of things, Done long ago and ill done." (*She halts.*) How can I go on, I cannot. Oh let me just flop down flat on the road like a big fat jelly out of a bowl and never move again! A great big slop thick with grit and dust and flies, they would have to scoop me up with a shovel. (*Pause.*) Heavens, there is that up mail again, what will become of me! (*The dragging steps resume.*) Oh I am just a hysterical old hag I know, destroyed with sorrow and pining and gentility and church-going and fat and rheumatism and childlessness. (*Pause. Brokenly.*) Minnie! Little Minnie! (*Pause.*) Love, that is all I asked, a little love, daily, twice daily, fifty years of twice daily love like a Paris horse-butcher's regular, what normal woman wants affection? A peck on the jaw at morning, near the ear, and another at evening, peck, peck, till you grow whiskers on you. There is that lovely laburnum again.
Dragging feet. Sound of bicycle-bell. It is old Mr.

9

*Tyler coming up behind her on his bicycle, on his
way to the station. Squeak of brakes. He slows
down and rides abreast of her.*

MR. TYLER: Mrs. Rooney! Pardon me if I do not doff my cap,
I'd fall off. Divine day for the meeting.

MRS. ROONEY: Oh, Mr. Tyler, you startled the life out of me
stealing up behind me like that like a deer-stalker!
Oh!

MR. TYLER: (*playfully*). I rang my bell, Mrs. Rooney, the
moment I sighted you I started tinkling my bell,
now don't you deny it.

MRS. ROONEY: Your bell is one thing, Mr. Tyler, and you are
another. What news of your poor daughter?

MR. TYLER: Fair, fair. They removed everything, you know,
the whole . . . er . . . bag of tricks. Now I am
grandchildless.
Dragging feet.

MRS. ROONEY: Gracious how you wobble! Dismount, for mercy's
sake, or ride on.

MR. TYLER: Perhaps if I were to lay my hand lightly on your
shoulder, Mrs. Rooney, how would that be?
(*Pause.*) Would you permit that?

MRS. ROONEY: No, Mr. Rooney, Mr. Tyler I mean, I am tired of
light old hands on my shoulders and other
senseless places, sick and tired of them. Heavens,
here comes Connolly's van! (*She halts. Sound of
motor-van. It approaches, passes with thunderous
rattles, recedes.*) Are you all right, Mr. Tyler?
(*Pause.*) Where is he? (*Pause.*) Ah there you are!
(*The dragging steps resume.*) That was a narrow
squeak.

MR. TYLER: I alit in the nick of time.

MRS. ROONEY: It is suicide to be abroad. But what is it to be
at home, Mr. Tyler, what is it to be at home? A

lingering dissolution. Now we are white with dust from head to foot. I beg your pardon?

MR. TYLER: Nothing, Mrs. Rooney, nothing, I was merely cursing, under my breath, God and man, under my breath, and the wet Saturday afternoon of my conception. My back tyre has gone down again. I pumped it hard as iron before I set out. And now I am on the rim.

MRS. ROONEY: Oh what a shame!

MR. TYLER: Now if it were the front I should not so much mind. But the back. The back! The chain! The oil! The grease! The hub! The brakes! The gear! No! It is too much!

Dragging steps.

MRS. ROONEY: Are we very late. Mr. Tyler? I have not the courage to look at my watch.

MR. TYLER: (*bitterly*). Late! I on my bicycle as I bowled along was already late. Now therefore we are doubly late, trebly, quadrupedly late. Would I had shot by you, without a word.

Dragging feet.

MRS. ROONEY: Whom are you meeting, Mr. Tyler?

MR. TYLER: Hardy. (*Pause.*) We used to climb together. (*Pause.*) I saved his life once. (*Pause.*) I have not forgotten it.

Dragging feet. They stop.

MRS. ROONEY: Let us halt a moment and let this vile dust fall back upon the viler worms.

Silence. Rural sounds.

MR. TYLER: What sky! What light! Ah in spite of all it is a blessed thing to be alive in such weather, and out of hospital.

MRS. ROONEY: Alive?

MR. TYLER: Well half alive shall we say?

MRS. ROONEY: Speak for yourself, Mr. Tyler. I am not half alive
nor anything approaching it. (*Pause.*) What are we
standing here for? This dust will not settle in our
time. And when it does some great roaring
machine will come and whirl it all skyhigh again.

MR. TYLER: Well, shall we be getting along in that case?

MRS. ROONEY: No.

MR. TYLER: Come, Mrs. Rooney——

MRS. ROONEY: Go, Mr. Tyler, go on and leave me, listening to
the cooing of the ringdoves. (*Cooing.*) If you see
my poor blind Dan tell him I was on my way to
meet him when it all come over me again, like a
flood. Say to him, Your poor wife, she told me to
tell you it all came flooding over her again and . . .
(*the voice breaks*) . . . she simply went back home
. . . straight back home . . .

MR. TYLER: Come, Mrs. Rooney, come, the mail has not yet
gone up, just take my free arm and we'll be there
with time and to spare.

MRS. ROONEY: (*sobbing*). What? What's all this now? (*Calmer.*)
Can't you see I'm in trouble? (*With anger.*)
Have you no respect for misery? (*Sobbing.*)
Minnie! Little Minnie!

MR. TYLER: Come, Mrs. Rooney, come, the mail has not yet
gone up, just take my free arm and we'll be there
with time and to spare.

MRS. ROONEY: (*brokenly*). In her forties now she'd be, I don't
know, fifty girding up her lovely little loins,
getting ready for the change . . .

MR. TYLER: Come, Mrs. Rooney, come, the mail——

MRS. ROONEY: (*exploding*). Will you get along with you, Mr.
Rooney, Mr. Tyler I mean, will you get along with
you now and cease molesting me? What kind of a
country is this where a woman can't weep her

heart out on the highways and byways without
being tormented by retired bill-brokers! (*Mr.
Tyler prepares to mount his bicycle.*) Heavens you're
not going to ride her flat! (*Mr. Tyler mounts.*)
You'll tear your tube to ribbons! (*Mr. Tyler rides
off. Receding sound of bumping bicycle. Silence.
Cooing.*) Venus birds! Billing in the woods all the
long summer long. (*Pause.*) Oh cursed corset! If I
could let it out, without indecent exposure. Mr.
Tyler! Mr. Tyler! Come back and unlace me
behind the hedge! (*She laughs wildly, ceases.*)
What's wrong with me, what's wrong with me,
never tranquil, seething out of my dirty old pelt,
out of my skull, oh to be in atoms, in atoms!
(*Frenziedly.*) ATOMS! (*Silence. Cooing. Faintly.*)
Jesus! (*Pause.*) Jesus!
*Sound of car coming up behind her. It slows down
and draws up beside her, engine running. It is Mr.
Slocum, the Clerk of the Racecourse.*

MR. SLOCUM: Is anything wrong, Mrs. Rooney? You are bent
all double. Have you a pain in the stomach?
Silence. Mrs. Rooney laughs wildly. Finally.

MRS. ROONEY: Well if it isn't my old admirer the Clerk of the
Course, in his limousine.

MR. SLOCUM: May I offer you a lift, Mrs. Rooney? Are you
going in my direction?

MRS. ROONEY: I am, Mr. Slocum, we all are. (*Pause.*) How is
your poor mother?

MR. SLOCUM: Thank you, she is fairly comfortable. We manage
to keep her out of pain. That is the great thing,
Mrs. Rooney, is it not?

MRS. ROONEY: Yes, indeed, Mr. Slocum, that is the great thing,
I don't know how you do it. (*Pause. She slaps her
cheek violently.*) Ah these wasps!

13

MR. SLOCUM: (*coolly*). May I then offer you a seat, Madam?
MRS. ROONEY: (*with exaggerated enthusiasm*). Oh that would be heavenly, Mr. Slocum, just simply heavenly. (*Dubiously.*) But would I ever get in, you look very high off the ground today, these new balloon tyres I presume. (*Sound of door opening and Mrs. Rooney trying to get in.*) Does this roof never come off? No? (*Efforts of Mrs. Rooney.*) No . . . I'll never do it . . . you'll have to get down, Mr. Slocum, and help me from the rear. (*Pause.*) What was that? (*Pause. Aggrieved.*) This is all your suggestion, Mr. Slocum, not mine. Drive on, Sir, drive on.
MR. SLOCUM: (*switching off the engine*). I'm coming, Mrs. Rooney, I'm coming, give me time, I'm as stiff as yourself.
Sound of Mr. Slocum extracting himself from driver's seat.
MRS. ROONEY: Stiff! Well I like that! And me heaving all over back and front. (*To herself.*) The dry old reprobate!
MR. SLOCUM: (*on position behind her*). Now, Mrs. Rooney, how shall we do this?
MRS. ROONEY: As if I were a bale, Mr. Slocum, don't be afraid. (*Pause. Sounds of effort.*) That's the way! (*Effort.*) Lower! (*Effort.*) Wait! (*Pause.*) No, don't let go! (*Pause.*) Suppose I do get up, will I ever get down?
MR. SLOCUM: (*breathing hard*). You'll get down, Mrs. Rooney, you'll get down. We may not get you up, but I warrant you we'll get you down.
He resumes his efforts. Sound of these.
MRS. ROONEY: Oh! . . . Lower! . . . Don't be afraid! . . . We're past the age when . . . There! . . . Now! . . . Get

14

your shoulder under it ... Oh! ... (*Giggles.*) Oh glory! ... Up! Up! ... Ah! ... I'm in! (*Panting of Mr. Slocum. He slams the door. In a scream.*) My frock! You've nipped my frock! (*Mr. Slocum opens the door. Mrs. Rooney frees her frock. Mr. Slocum slams the door. His violent unintelligible muttering as he walks round to the other door. Tearfully.*) My nice frock! Look what you've done to my nice frock! (*Mr. Slocum gets into his seat, slam's driver's door, presses starter. The engine does not start. He releases starter.*) What will Dan say when he sees me?

MR. SLOCUM: Has he then recovered his sight?

MRS. ROONEY: No, I mean when he knows, what will he say when he feels the hole? (*Mr. Slocum presses starter. As before. Silence.*) What are you doing, Mr. Slocum?

MR. SLOCUM: Gazing straight before me, Mrs. Rooney, through the windscreen, into the void.

MRS. ROONEY: Start her up, I beseech you, and let us be off. This is awful!

MR. SLOCUM: (*dreamily*). All morning she went like a dream and now she is dead. That is what you get for a good deed. (*Pause. Hopefully.*) Perhaps if I were to choke her. (*He does so, presses the starter. The engine roars. Roaring to make himself heard.*) She was getting too much air!
He throttles down, grinds in his first gear, moves off, changes up in a grinding of gears.

MRS. ROONEY: (*in anguish*). Mind the hen! (*Scream of brakes. Squawk of hen.*) Oh, mother, you have squashed her, drive on, drive on! (*The car accelerates. Pause.*) What a death! One minute picking happy at the dung, on the road, in the sun, with now and then a dust bath, and then—bang!—all her troubles

15

over. (*Pause*.) All the laying and the hatching.
(*Pause*.) Just one great squawk and then . . . peace.
(*Pause*.) They would have slit her weasand in any
case. (*Pause*.) Here we are, let me down. (*The car
slows down, stops, engine running. Mr. Slocum blows
his horn. Pause. Louder. Pause*.) What are you up
to now, Mr. Slocum? We are at a standstill, all
danger is past and you blow your horn. Now if
instead of blowing it now you had blown it at that
unfortunate——
*Horn violently. Tommy the porter appears at top of
station steps.*

MR. SLOCUM: (*calling*). Will you come down, Tommy, and help
this lady out, she's stuck. (*Tommy descends the
steps*.) Open the door, Tommy, and ease her out.
Tommy opens the door.

TOMMY: Certainly, sir. Nice day for the races, sir. What
would you fancy for——

MRS. ROONEY: Don't mind me. Don't take any notice of me. I do
not exist. The fact is well known.

MR. SLOCUM: Do as you're asked, Tommy, for the love of God.

TOMMY: Yessir. Now, Mrs. Rooney.
He starts pulling her out.

MRS. ROONEY: Wait, Tommy, wait now, don't bustle me, just let
me wheel round and get my feet to the ground.
(*Her efforts to achieve this*.) Now.

TOMMY: (*pulling her out*). Mind your feather, Ma'am.
(*Sounds of effort*.) Easy now, easy.

MRS. ROONEY: Wait, for God's sake, you'll have me beheaded.

TOMMY: Crouch down, Mrs. Rooney, crouch down, and
get your head in the open.

MRS. ROONEY: Crouch down! At my time of life! This is lunacy!

TOMMY: Press her down, sir.
Sounds of combined efforts.

MRS. ROONEY: Pity!

TOMMY: Now! She's coming! Straighten up, Ma'am! There! *Mr. Slocum slams the door.*

MRS. ROONEY: Am I out?
The voice of Mr. Barrell, the station-master, raised in anger.

MR. BARRELL: Tommy! Tommy! Where the hell is he?
Mr. Slocum grinds in his gear.

TOMMY: (*hurriedly*). You wouldn't have something for the Ladies Plate, sir? I was given Flash Harry.

MR. SLOCUM: (*scornfully*). Flash Harry! That carthorse!

MR. BARRELL: (*at top of steps, roaring*). Tommy! Blast your bleeding bloody—(*He sees Mrs. Rooney.*) Oh, Mrs. Rooney ... (*Mr. Slocum drives away in a grinding of gears.*) Who's that crucifying his gearbox, Tommy?

TOMMY: Old Cissy Slocum.

MRS. ROONEY: Cissy Slocum! That's a nice way to refer to your betters. Cissy Slocum! And you an orphan!

MR. BARRELL: (*angrily to Tommy*). What are you doing stravaging down here on the public road? This is no place for you at all! Nip up there on the platform now and whip out the truck! Won't the twelve thirty be on top of us before we can turn round?

TOMMY: (*bitterly*). And that's the thanks you get for a Christian act.

MR. BARRELL: (*violently*). Get on with you now before I report you! (*Slow feet of Tommy climbing steps.*) Do you want me to come down to you with the shovel? (*The feet quicken, recede, cease.*) Ah God forgive me, it's a hard life. (*Pause.*) Well, Mrs. Rooney, it's nice to see you up and about again. You were laid up there a long time.

MRS. ROONEY: Not long enough, Mr. Barrell. (*Pause.*) Would I were still in bed, Mr. Barrell. (*Pause.*) Would I were lying stretched out in my comfortable bed, Mr. Barrell, just wasting slowly, painlessly away, keeping up my strength with arrowroot and calves-foot jelly, till in the end you wouldn't see me under the blankets any more than a board. (*Pause.*) Oh no coughing or spitting or bleeding or vomiting, just drifting gently down into the higher life, and remembering, remembering . . . (*the voice breaks*) . . . all the silly unhappiness . . . as though . . . it had never happened . . . What did I do with that handkerchief? (*Sound of handkerchief loudly applied.*) How long have you been master of this station now, Mr. Barrell?

MR. BARRELL: Don't ask me, Mrs. Rooney, don't ask me.

MRS. ROONEY: You stepped into your father's shoes, I believe, when he took them off.

MR. BARRELL: Poor Pappy! (*Reverent pause.*) He didn't live long to enjoy his ease.

MRS. ROONEY: I remember him clearly. A small ferrety purple-faced widower, deaf as a doornail, very testy and snappy. (*Pause.*) I suppose you'll be retiring soon yourself, Mr. Barrell, and growing your roses. (*Pause.*) Did I understand you to say the twelve thirty would soon be upon us?

MR. BARRELL: Those were my words.

MRS. ROONEY: But according to my watch which is more or less right—or was—by the eight o'clock news the time is now coming up to twelve . . . (*pause as she consults her watch*) . . . thirty-six. (*Pause.*) And yet upon the other hand the up mail has not yet gone through. (*Pause.*) Or has it sped by unbeknown to me? (*Pause.*) For there was a moment there, I

remember now, I was so plunged in sorrow I wouldn't have heard a steam roller go over me. (*Pause. Mr. Barrell turns to go.*) Don't go, Mr. Barrell! (*Mr. Barrell goes. Loud.*) Mr. Barrell! (*Pause. Louder.*) Mr. Barrell!
Mr. Barrell comes back.

MR. BARRELL: (*testily*). What is it, Mrs. Rooney, I have my work to do.
Silence. Sound of wind.

MRS. ROONEY: The wind is getting up. (*Pause. Wind.*) The best of the day is over. (*Pause. Wind. Dreamily.*) Soon the rain will begin to fall and go on falling, all afternoon. (*Mr. Barrell goes.*) Then at evening the clouds will part, the setting sun will shine an instant, then sink, behind the hills. (*She realizes Mr. Barrell has gone.*) Mr. Barrell! Mr. Barrell! (*Silence.*) I estrange them all. They come towards me, uninvited, bygones bygones, full of kindness, anxious to help . . . (*the voice breaks*) . . . genuinely pleased . . . to see me again . . . looking so well . . . (*Handkerchief.*) A few simple words . . . from my heart . . . and I am all alone . . . once more . . . (*Handkerchief. Vehemently.*) I should not be out at all! I should never leave the grounds! (*Pause.*) Oh there is that Fitt woman, I wonder will she bow to me. (*Sound of Miss Fitt approaching, humming a hymn. She starts climbing the steps.*) Miss Fitt! (*Miss Fitt halts, stops humming.*) Am I then invisible, Miss Fitt? Is this cretonne so becoming to me that I merge into the masonry? (*Miss Fitt descends a step.*) That is right, Miss Fitt, look closely and you will finally distinguish a once female shape.

MISS FITT: Mrs. Rooney! I saw you, but I did not know you.

MRS. ROONEY: Last Sunday we worshipped together. We knelt side by side at the same altar. We drank from the same chalice. Have I so changed since then?

MISS FITT: (*shocked*). Oh but in church, Mrs. Rooney, in church I am alone with my Maker. Are not you? (*Pause.*) Why even the sexton himself, you know, when he takes up the collection, knows it is useless to pause before me. I simply do not see the plate, or bag, whatever it is they use, how could I? (*Pause.*) Why even when all is over and I go out into the sweet fresh air, why even then for the first furlong or so I stumble in a kind of daze as you might say, oblivious to my co-religionists. And they are very kind I must admit—the vast majority —very kind and understanding. They know me now and take no umbrage. There she goes, they say, there goes the dark Miss Fitt, alone with her Maker, take no notice of her. And they step down off the path to avoid my running into them. (*Pause.*) Ah yes, I am distray, very distray, even on week-days. Ask Mother, if you do not believe me. Hetty, she says, when I start eating my doily instead of the thin bread and butter. Hetty, how can you be so distray? (*Sighs.*) I suppose the truth is I am not there, Mrs. Rooney, just not really there at all. I see, hear, smell, and so on, I go through the usual motions, but my heart is not in it, Mrs. Rooney, but heart is in none of it. Left to myself, with no one to check me, I would soon be flown . . . home. (*Pause.*) So if you think I cut you just now, Mrs. Rooney, you do me an injustice. All I saw was a big pale blur, just another big pale blur. (*Pause.*) Is anything amiss, Mrs. Rooney, you do not look normal somehow. So bowed and bent.

20

MRS. ROONEY: (*ruefully*). Maddy Rooney, née Dunne, the big
pale blur. (*Pause.*) You have piercing sight, Miss
Fitt, if you only knew it, literally piercing.
Pause.

MISS FITT: Well . . . is there anything I can do, now that I am
here?

MRS. ROONEY: If you would help me up the face of this cliff,
Miss Fitt, I have little doubt your Maker would
requite you, if no one else.

MISS FITT: Now, now, Mrs. Rooney, don't put your teeth in
me. Requite! I make these sacrifices for nothing—
or not at all. (*Pause. Sound of her descending steps.*)
I take it you want to lean on me, Mrs. Rooney.

MRS. ROONEY: I asked Mr. Barrell to give me his arm, just give
me his arm. (*Pause.*) He turned on his heel and
strode away.

MISS FITT: Is it my arm you want then? (*Pause. Impatiently.*)
Is it my arm you want, Mrs. Rooney, or what is it?

MRS. ROONEY: (*exploding*). Your arm! Any arm! A helping hand!
For five seconds! Christ what a planet!

MISS FITT: Really . . . Do you know what it is, Mrs. Rooney,
I do not think it is wise of you to be going about
at all.

MRS. ROONEY: (*violently*). Come down here, Miss Fitt, and give
me your arm, before I scream down the parish!
*Pause. Wind. Sound of Miss Fitt descending last
steps.*

MISS FITT: (*resignedly*). Well, I suppose it is the Protestant
thing to do.

MRS. ROONEY: Pismires do it for one another. (*Pause.*) I have
seen slugs do it. (*Miss Fitt proffers her arm.*) No,
the other side, my dear, if it's all the same to you,
I'm left-handed on top of everything else. (*She
takes Miss Fitt's right arm.*) Heavens, child, you're

just a bag of bones, you need building up. (*Sound of her toiling up steps on Miss Fitt's arm.*) This is worse than the Matterhorn, were you ever up the Matterhorn, Miss Fitt, great honeymoon resort. (*Sound of toiling.*) Why don't they have a handrail? (*Panting.*) Wait till I get some air. (*Pause.*) Don't let me go! (*Miss Fitt hums her hymn. After a moment Mrs. Rooney joins in with the words.*) . . . the encircling gloo-oom . . . (*Miss Fitt stops humming*) . . . tum tum me on. (*Forte.*) The night is dark and I am far from ho-ome, tum tum——

MISS FITT: (*hysterically*). Stop it, Mrs. Rooney, stop it, or I'll drop you!

MRS. ROONEY: Wasn't it that they sung on the *Lusitania*? Or Rock of Ages? Most touching it must have been. Or was it the *Titanic*?
Attracted by the noise a group, including Mr. Tyler, Mr. Barrell and Tommy, gathers at top of steps.

MR. BARRELL: What the——
Silence.

MR. TYLER: Lovely day for the fixture.
Loud titter from Tommy cut short by Mr. Barrell with backhanded blow in the stomach. Appropriate noise from Tommy.

Female Voice: (*shrill*). Oh look, Dolly, look!

DOLLY: What, Mamma?

Female Voice: They are stuck! (*Cackling laugh.*) They are stuck!

MRS. ROONEY: Now we are the laughing-stock of the twenty-six counties. Or is it thirty-six?

MR. TYLER: That is a nice way to treat your defenceless subordinates, Mr. Barrell, hitting them without warning in the pit of the stomach.

MISS FITT: Has anybody seen my mother?

MR. BARRELL: Who is that?

TOMMY: The dark Miss Fitt.

MR. BARRELL: Where is her face?

MRS. ROONEY: Now, deary, I am ready if you are. (*They toil up remaining steps.*) Stand back, you cads!
Shuffle of feet.

Female Voice: Mind yourself, Dolly!

MRS. ROONEY: Thank you, Miss Fitt, thank you, that will do, just prop me up against the wall like a roll of tarpaulin and that will be all, for the moment. (*Pause.*) I am sorry for all this ramdam, Miss Fitt, had I known you were looking for your mother I should not have importuned you, I know what it is.

MR. TYLER: (*in marvelling aside*). Ramdam!

Female Voice: Come, Dolly darling, let us take up our stand before the first class smokers. Give me your hand and hold me tight, one can be sucked under.

MR. TYLER: You have lost your mother, Miss Fitt?

MISS FITT: Good morning, Mr. Tyler.

MR. TYLER: Good morning, Miss Fitt.

MR. BARRELL: Good morning, Miss Fitt.

MISS FITT: Good morning, Mr. Barrell.

MR. TYLER: You have lost your mother, Miss Fitt?

MISS FITT: She said she would be on the last train.

MRS. ROONEY: Do not imagine, because I am silent, that I am not present, and alive, to all that is going on.

MR. TYLER: (*to Miss Fitt*). When you say the last train——

MRS. ROONEY: Do not flatter yourselves for one moment, because I hold aloof, that my sufferings have ceased. No. The entire scene, the hills, the plain, the race-course with its miles and miles of white rails and three red stands, the pretty little wayside station, even you yourselves, yes, I mean it, and over all the clouding blue, I see it all, I stand here and see it all with eyes . . . (*the voice breaks*) . . .

23

through eyes . . . oh if you had my eyes . . . you
would understand . . . the things they have seen
. . . and not looked away . . . this is nothing . . .
nothing . . . what did I do with that handkerchief?
Pause.

MR. TYLER: *(to Miss Fitt).* When you say the last train—*(Mrs.
Rooney blows her nose violently and long)*—when
you say the last train, Miss Fitt, I take it you mean
the twelve thirty.

MISS FITT: What else could I mean, Mr. Tyler, what else
could I *conceivably* mean?

MR. TYLER: Then you have no cause for anxiety, Miss Fitt, for
the twelve thirty has not yet arrived. Look. *(Miss
Fitt looks.)* No, up the line. *(Miss Fitt looks.
Patiently.)* No, Miss Fitt, follow the direction of
my index. *(Miss Fitt looks.)* There. You see now.
The signal. At the bawdy hour of nine. *(In rueful
afterthought.)* Or three alas! *(Mr. Barrell stifles a
guffaw.)* Thank you, Mr. Barrell.

MISS FITT: But the time is now getting on for——

MR. TYLER: *(patiently).* We all know, Miss Fitt, we all know
only too well what the time is now getting on for,
and yet the cruel fact remains that the twelve
thirty has not yet arrived.

MISS FITT: Not an accident, I trust! *(Pause.)* Do not tell me
she has left the track! *(Pause.)* Oh darling mother!
With the fresh sole for lunch!
*Loud titter from Tommy, checked as before by Mr.
Barrell.*

MR. BARRELL: That's enough old guff out of you. Nip up to the
box now and see has Mr. Case anything for me.
Tommy goes.

MRS. ROONEY: Poor Dan!

MISS FITT: *(in anguish).* What terrible thing has happened?

24

MR. TYLER: Now now, Miss Fitt, do not——

MRS. ROONEY: (*with vehement sadness*). Poor Dan!

MR. TYLER: Now now, Miss Fitt, do not give way . . . to
despair, all will come right . . . in the end. (*Aside
to Mr. Barrell.*) What *is* the situation, Mr. Barrell?
Not a collision surely?

MRS. ROONEY: (*enthusiastically*). A collision! Oh that would be
wonderful!

MISS FITT: (*horrified*). A collision! I knew it!

MR. TYLER: Come, Miss Fitt, let us move a little up the
platform.

MRS. ROONEY: Yes, let us all do that. (*Pause.*) No? (*Pause.*) You
have changed your mind? (*Pause.*) I quite agree,
we are better here, in the shadow of the waiting-
room.

MR. BARRELL: Excuse me a moment.

MRS. ROONEY: Before you slink away, Mr. Barrell, please, a state-
ment of some kind, I insist. Even the slowest train
on this brief line is not ten minutes and more
behind its scheduled time without good cause, one
imagines. (*Pause.*) We all know your station is the
best kept of the entire network, but there are times
when that is not enough, just not enough. (*Pause.*)
Now, Mr. Barrell, leave off chewing your
whiskers, we are waiting to hear from you—we the
unfortunate ticket-holders' nearest if not dearest.
Pause.

MR. TYLER: (*reasonably*). I do think we are owed some kind of
explanation, Mr. Barrell, if only to set our minds
at rest.

MR. BARRELL: I know nothing. All I know is there has been a
hitch. All traffic is retarded.

MRS. ROONEY: (*derisively*). Retarded! A hitch! Ah these celibates!
Here we are eating our hearts out with anxiety for

our loved ones and he calls that a hitch! Those of us like myself with heart and kidney trouble may collapse at any moment and he calls that a hitch! In our ovens the Saturday roast is burning to a shrivel and he calls that——

MR. TYLER: Here comes Tommy, running! I am glad I have been spared to see this.

TOMMY: (*excitedly, in the distance*). She's coming. (*Pause. Nearer.*) She's at the level-crossing!
Immediately exaggerated station sounds. Falling signals. Bells. Whistles. Crescendo of train whistle approaching. Sound of train rushing through station.

MRS. ROONEY: (*above rush of train*). The up mail! The up mail! (*The up mail recedes, the down train approaches, enters the station, pulls up with great hissing of steam and clashing of couplings. Noise of passengers descending, doors banging, Mr. Barrell shouting "Boghill! Boghill!", etc. Piercingly.*) Dan! .. Are you all right? ... Where is he? ... Dan! ... Did you see my husband? ... Dan! ... (*Noise of station emptying. Guard's whistle. Train departing, receding. Silence.*) He isn't on it! The misery I have endured, to get here, and he isn't on it! ... Mr. Barrell! ... Was he not on it? (*Pause.*) Is anything the matter, you look as if you had seen a ghost. (*Pause.*) Tommy! . . . Did you see the master?

TOMMY: He'll be along, Ma'am, Jerry is minding him.
Mr. Rooney suddenly appears on platform, advancing on small boy Jerry's arm. He is blind, thumps the ground with his stick and pants incessantly.

MRS. ROONEY: Oh, Dan! There you are! (*Her dragging feet as she hastens towards him. She reaches him. They halt.*) Where in the world were you?

MR. ROONEY: (*coolly*). Maddy.

MRS. ROONEY: Where were you all this time?

MR. ROONEY: In the men's.

MRS. ROONEY: Kiss me!

MR. ROONEY: Kiss you? In public? On the platform? Before the boy? Have you taken leave of your senses?

MRS. ROONEY: Jerry wouldn't mind. Would you, Jerry?

JERRY: No, Ma'am.

MRS. ROONEY: How is your poor father?

JERRY: They took him away, Ma'am.

MRS. ROONEY: Then you are all alone?

JERRY: Yes, Ma'am.

MR. ROONEY: Why are you here? You did not notify me.

MRS. ROONEY: I wanted to give you a surprise. For your birthday.

MR. ROONEY: My birthday?

MRS. ROONEY: Don't you remember? I wished you your happy returns in the bathroom.

MR. ROONEY: I did not hear you.

MRS. ROONEY: But I gave you a tie! You have it on!
Pause.

MR. ROONEY: How old am I now?

MRS. ROONEY: Now never mind about that. Come.

MR. ROONEY: Why did you not cancel the boy? Now we shall have to give him a penny.

MRS. ROONEY: (*miserably*). I forgot! I had such a time getting here! Such horrid nasty people! (*Pause. Pleading.*) Be nice to me, Dan, be nice to me today!

MR. ROONEY: Give the boy a penny.

MRS. ROONEY: Here are two halfpennies, Jerry. Run along now and buy yourself a nice gobstopper.

JERRY: Yes, Ma'am.

MR. ROONEY: Come for me on Monday, if I am still alive.

JERRY: Yessir.
He runs off.

27

MR. ROONEY: We could have saved sixpence. We have saved fivepence. (*Pause.*) But at what cost?
They move off along platform arm in arm. Dragging feet, panting, thudding stick.

MRS. ROONEY: Are you not well?
They halt, on Mr. Rooney's initiative.

MR. ROONEY: Once and for all, do not ask me to speak and move at the same time. I shall not say this in this life again.
They move off. Dragging feet, etc. They halt at top of steps.

MRS. ROONEY: Are you not——

MR. ROONEY: Let us get this precipice over.

MRS. ROONEY: Put your arm around me.

MR. ROONEY: Have you been drinking again? (*Pause.*) You are quivering like a blanc-mange. (*Pause.*) Are you in a condition to lead me? (*Pause.*) We shall fall into the ditch.

MRS. ROONEY: Oh, Dan! It will be like old times!

MR. ROONEY: Pull yourself together or I shall send Tommy for the cab. Then instead of having saved sixpence, no, fivepence, we shall have lost . . . (*calculating mumble*) . . . two and three less six one and no plus one one and no plus three one and nine and one ten and three two and one . . . (*normal voice*) two and one, we shall be the poorer to the tune of two and one. (*Pause.*) Curse that sun, it has gone in. What is the day doing?
Wind.

MRS. ROONEY: Shrouding, shrouding, the best of it is past. (*Pause.*) Soon the first great drops will fall slashing in the dust.

MR. ROONEY: And yet the glass was firm. (*Pause.*) Let us hasten home and sit before the fire. We shall draw the

blinds. You will read to me. I think Effie is going
to commit adultery with the Major. (*Brief drag of
feet.*) Wait! (*Feet cease. Stick tapping at steps.*) I
have been up and down these steps five thousand
times and still I do not know how many there are.
When I think there are six there are four or five or
seven or eight and when I remember there are five
there are three or four or six or seven and when
finally I realize there are seven there are five or
six or eight or nine. Sometimes I wonder if they
do not change them in the night. (*Pause.
Irritably.*) Well? How many do you make them
today?

MRS. ROONEY: Do not ask me to count, Dan, not now.

MR. ROONEY: Not count! One of the few satisfactions in life!

MRS. ROONEY: Not steps. Dan, please, I always get them wrong.
Then you might fall on your wound and I would
have that on my manure-heap on top of everything
else. No, just cling to me and all will be well.
*Confused noise of their descent. Panting, stumbling,
ejaculations, curses. Silence.*

MR. ROONEY: Well! That is what you call well!

MRS. ROONEY: We are down. And little the worse. (*Silence. A
donkey brays. Silence.*) That was a true donkey. Its
father and mother were donkeys.
Silence.

MR. ROONEY: Do you know what it is, I think I shall retire.

MRS. ROONEY: (*appalled*). Retire! And live at home? On your
grant!

MR. ROONEY: Never tread these cursed steps again. Trudge this
hellish road for the last time. Sit at home on the
remnants of my bottom counting the hours—till
the next meal. (*Pause.*) The very thought puts life
in me! Forward, before it dies!

29

They move on. Dragging feet, panting, thudding stick.

MRS. ROONEY: Now mind, here is the path ... Up! ... Well done! Now we are in safety and a straight run home.

MR. ROONEY: (*without halting, between gasps*). A straight ... run! ... She calls that ... a straight ... run! ...

MRS. ROONEY: Hush! Do not speak as you go along, you know it is not good for your coronary. (*Dragging steps, etc.*) Just concentrate on putting one foot before the next or whatever the expression is. (*Dragging feet, etc.*) That is the way, now we are doing nicely. (*Dragging feet, etc. They suddenly halt, on Mrs. Rooney's initiative.*) Heavens! I knew there was something! With all the excitement! I forgot!

MR. ROONEY: (*quietly*). Good God.

MRS. ROONEY: But you must know, Dan, of course, you were on it. Whatever happened? Tell me!

MR. ROONEY: I have never known anything to happen.

MRS. ROONEY: But you must——

MR. ROONEY: (*violently*). All this stopping and starting again is devilish, devilish! I get a little way on me and begin to be carried along when suddenly you stop dead! Two hundred pounds of unhealthy fat! What possessed you to come out at all? Let go of me!

MRS. ROONEY: (*in great agitation*). No, I must know, we won't stir from here till you tell me. Fifteen minutes late! On a thirty minute run! It's unheard of!

MR. ROONEY: I know nothing. Let go of me before I shake you off.

MRS. ROONEY: But you must know! You were on it! Was it at the terminus? Did you leave on time? Or was it on the

line? (*Pause.*) Did something happen on the line?
(*Pause.*) Dan! (*Brokenly.*) Why won't you tell me!
Silence. They move off. Dragging feet, etc. They
halt. Pause.

MR. ROONEY: Poor Maddy! (*Pause. Children's cries.*) What was
that?
Pause for Mrs. Rooney to ascertain.

MRS. ROONEY: The Lynch twins jeering at us.
Cries.

MR. ROONEY: Will they pelt us with mud today, do you
suppose?
Cries.

MRS. ROONEY: Let us turn and face them. (*Cries. They turn.*
Silence.) Threaten them with your stick. (*Silence.*)
They have run away.
Pause.

MR. ROONEY: Did you ever wish to kill a child? (*Pause.*) Nip
some young doom in the bud. (*Pause.*) Many a
time at night, in winter, on the black road home,
I nearly attacked the boy. (*Pause.*) Poor Jerry!
(*Pause.*) What restrained me then? (*Pause.*) Not
fear of man. (*Pause.*) Shall we go on backwards
now a little?

MRS. ROONEY: Backwards?

MR. ROONEY: Yes. Or you forwards and I backwards. The perfect pair. Like Dante's damned, with their faces
arsy-versy. Our tears will water our bottoms.

MRS. ROONEY: What is the matter, Dan? Are you not well?

MR. ROONEY: Well! Did you ever know me to be well? The day
you met me I should have been in bed. The day
you proposed to me the doctors gave me up. You
knew that, did you not? The night you married
me they came for me with an ambulance. You have
not forgotten that, I suppose? (*Pause.*) No, I

31

cannot be said to be well. But I am no worse. Indeed I am better than I was. The loss of my sight was a great fillip. If I could go deaf and dumb I think I might pant on to be a hundred. Or have I done so? (*Pause.*) Was I a hundred today? (*Pause.*) Am I a hundred, Maddy?
Silence

MRS. ROONEY: All is still. No living soul in sight. There is no one to ask. The world is feeding. The wind— (*brief wind*)—scarcely stirs the leaves and the birds—(*brief chirp*)—are tired singing. The cows —(*brief moo*)—and sheep—(*brief baa*)—ruminate in silence. The dogs—(*brief bark*)—are hushed and the hens—(*brief cackle*)—sprawl torpid in the dust. We are alone. There is no one to ask.
Silence.

MR. ROONEY: (*clearing his throat, narrative tone*). We drew out on the tick of time, I can vouch for that. I was——

MRS. ROONEY: How can you vouch for it?

MR. ROONEY: (*normal tone, angrily*). I can vouch for it, I tell you! Do you want my relation or don't you? (*Pause. Narrative tone.*) On the tick of time. I had the compartment to myself, as usual. At least I hope so, for I made no attempt to restrain myself. My mind—(*Normal tone.*) But why do we not sit down somewhere? Are we afraid we should never rise again?

MRS. ROONEY: Sit down on what?

MR. ROONEY: On a bench, for example.

MRS. ROONEY: There is no bench.

MR. ROONEY: Then on a bank, let us sink down upon a bank.

MRS. ROONEY: There is no bank.

MR. ROONEY: Then we cannot. (*Pause.*) I dream of other roads, in other lands. Of another home, another—(*he*

32

hesitates)—another home. (*Pause.*) What was **I**
trying to say?

MR. ROONEY: Something about your mind.

MRS. ROONEY: (*startled*). My mind? Are you sure. (*Pause.
Incredulous.*) My mind? ... (*Pause.*) Ah yes.
(*Narrative tone.*) Alone in the compartment my
mind began to work, as so often after office hours,
on the way home, in the train, to the lilt of the
bogeys. Your season-ticket, I said, costs you
twelve pounds a year and you earn, on an average,
seven and six a day, that is to say barely enough to
keep you alive and twitching with the help of food,
drink, tobacco and periodicals until you finally
reach home and fall into bed. Add to this—or
subtract from it—rent, stationery, various sub-
scriptions, tramfares to and fro, light and heat,
permits and licences, hairtrims and shaves, tips to
escorts, upkeep of premises and appearances, and
a thousand unspecifiable sundries, and it is clear
that by lying at home in bed, day and night, winter
and summer, with a change of pyjamas once a
fortnight, you would add very considerably to
your income. Business, I said—(*A cry. Pause.
Again. Normal tone.*) Did I hear a cry?

MRS. ROONEY: Mrs. Tully I fancy. Her poor husband is in con-
stant pain and beats her unmercifully.
Silence.

MR. ROONEY: That was a short knock. (*Pause.*) What was I
trying to get at?

MRS. ROONEY: Business.

MR. ROONEY: Ah yes, business. (*Narrative tone.*) Business, old
man, I said, retire from business, it has retired
from you. (*Normal tone.*) One has these moments
of lucidity.

33

MRS. ROONEY: I feel very cold and weak.

MR. ROONEY: (*narrative tone*). On the other hand, I said, there are the horrors of home life, the dusting, sweeping, airing, scrubbing, waxing, waning, washing, mangling, drying, mowing, clipping, raking, rolling, scuffling, shovelling, grinding, tearing, pounding, banging and slamming. And the brats, the happy little healthy little howling neighbours' brats. Of all this and much more the week-end, the Saturday intermission and then the day of rest, have given you some idea. But what must it be like on a working-day? A Wednesday? A Friday! What must it be like on a Friday! And I fell to thinking of my silent, backstreet, basement office, with its obliterated plate, rest-couch and velvet hangings, and what it means to be buried there alive, if only from ten to five, with convenient to the one hand a bottle of light pale ale and to the other a long ice-cold fillet of hake. Nothing, I said, not even fully certified death, can ever take the place of that. It was then I noticed we were at a standstill. (*Pause. Normal tone. Irritably.*) Why are you hanging out of me like that? Have you swooned away?

MRS. ROONEY: I feel very cold and faint. The wind—(*whistling wind*)—is whistling through my summer frock as if I had nothing on over my bloomers. I have had no solid food since my elevenses.

MR. ROONEY: You have ceased to care. I speak—and you listen to the wind.

MRS. ROONEY: No no, I am agog, tell me all, then we shall press on and never pause, never pause, till we come safe to haven.

Pause.

MR. ROONEY: Never pause . . . safe to haven . . . Do you know, Maddy, sometimes one would think you were struggling with a dead language.

MRS. ROONEY: Yes indeed, Dan, I know full well what you mean, I often have that feeling, it is unspeakably excruciating.

MR. ROONEY: I confess I have it sometimes myself, when I happen to overhear what I am saying.

MRS. ROONEY: Well, you know, it will be dead in time, just like our own poor dear Gaelic, there is that to be said. *Urgent baa.*

MR. ROONEY: *(startled).* Good God!

MRS. ROONEY: Oh the pretty little woolly lamb, crying to suck its mother! Theirs has not changed, since Arcady. *Pause.*

MR. ROONEY: Where was I in my composition?

MRS. ROONEY: At a standstill.

MR. ROONEY: Ah yes. *(Clears his throat. Narrative tone.)* I concluded naturally that we had entered a station and would soon be on our way again, and I sat on, without misgiving. Not a sound. Things are very dull today, I said, nobody getting down, nobody getting on. Then as time flew by and nothing happened I realized my error. We had not entered a station.

MRS. ROONEY: Did you not spring up and poke your head out of the window?

MR. ROONEY: What good would that have done me?

MRS. ROONEY: Why to call out to be told what was amiss.

MR. ROONEY: I did not care what was amiss. No, I just sat on, saying, If this train were never to move again I should not greatly mind. Then gradually a—how shall I say—a growing desire to—er—you know—

35

welled up within me. Nervous probably. In fact
now I am sure. You know, the feeling of being
confined.

MRS. ROONEY: Yes yes, I have been through that.

MR. ROONEY: If we sit here much longer, I said, I really do not
know what I shall do. I got up and paced to and
fro between the seats, like a caged beast.

MRS. ROONEY: That is a help sometimes.

MR. ROONEY: After what seemed an eternity we simply moved
off. And the next thing was Barrell bawling the
abhorred name. I got down and Jerry led me to
the men's, or Fir as they call it now, from Vir
Viris I suppose, the V becoming F, in accordance
with Grimm's Law. (*Pause.*) The rest you know.
(*Pause.*) You say nothing? (*Pause.*) Say something.
Maddy. Say you believe me.

MRS. ROONEY: I remember once attending a lecture by one of
these new mind doctors. I forget what you call
them. He spoke——

MR. ROONEY: A lunatic specialist?

MRS. ROONEY: No no, just the troubled mind. I was hoping he
might shed a little light on my lifelong preoccupa-
tion with horses' buttocks.

MR. ROONEY: A neurologist.

MRS. ROONEY: No no, just mental distress, the name will come
back to me in the night. I remember his telling us
the story of a little girl, very strange and unhappy
in her ways, and how he treated her unsuccessfully
over a period of years and was finally obliged to
give up the case. He could find nothing wrong
with her, he said. The only thing wrong with her
as far as he could see was that she was dying. And
she did in fact die, shortly after he washed his
hands of her.

36

MR. ROONEY: Well? What is there so wonderful about that?

MRS. ROONEY: No, it was just something he said, and the way he said it, that have haunted me ever since.

MR. ROONEY: You lie awake at night, tossing to and fro and brooding on it.

MRS. ROONEY: On it and other ... wretchedness. (*Pause.*) When he had done with the little girl he stood there motionless for some time, quite two minutes I should say, looking down at his table. Then he suddenly raised his head and exclaimed, as if he had had a revelation, The trouble with her was she had never been really born! (*Pause.*) He spoke throughout without notes. (*Pause.*) I left before the end.

MR. ROONEY: Nothing about your buttocks? (*Mrs. Rooney weeps. In affectionate remonstrance.*) Maddy!

MRS. ROONEY: There is nothing to be done for those people!

MR. ROONEY: For which is there? (*Pause.*) That does not sound right somehow. (*Pause.*) What way am I facing?

MRS. ROONEY: What?

MR. ROONEY: I have forgotten what way I am facing.

MRS. ROONEY: You have turned aside and are bowed down over the ditch.

MR. ROONEY: There is a dead dog down there.

MRS. ROONEY: No no, just the rotting leaves

MR. ROONEY: In June? Rotting leaves in June?

MRS. ROONEY: Yes, dear, from last year, and from the year before last, and from the year before that again. (*Silence. Rainy wind. They move on. Dragging steps, etc.*) There is that lovely laburnum again. Poor thing, it is losing all its tassels. (*Dragging steps, etc.*) There are the first drops. (*Rain. Dragging feet, etc.*) Golden drizzle. (*Dragging steps, etc.*) Do not mind me, dear, I am just talking to myself. *Rain*

37

heavier. Dragging steps, etc.) Can hinnies procreate, I wonder?
They halt.

MR. ROONEY: Say that again.

MRS. ROONEY: Come on, dear, don't mind me, we are getting
drenched.

MR. ROONEY: (*forcibly*). Can what what?

MRS. ROONEY: Hinnies procreate. (*Silence.*) You know, hinnies,
or jinnies, aren't they barren, or sterile, or whatever it is? (*Pause.*) It wasn't an ass's colt at all, you
know, I asked the Regius Professor.
Pause.

MR. ROONEY: He should know.

MRS. ROONEY: Yes, it was a hinny, he rode into Jerusalem or
wherever it was on a hinny. (*Pause.*) That must
mean something. (*Pause.*) It's like the sparrows,
than many of which we are of more value, they
weren't sparrows at all.

MR. ROONEY: Than many of which!... You exaggerate, Maddy.

MRS. ROONEY: (*with emotion*). They weren't sparrows at all!

MR. ROONEY: Does that put our price up?
*Silence. They move on. Wind and rain. Dragging
feet, etc. They halt.*

MRS. ROONEY: Do you want some dung? (*Silence. They move on.
Wind and rain, etc. They halt.*) Why do you stop?
Do you want to say something?

MR. ROONEY: No.

MRS. ROONEY: Then why do you stop?

MR. ROONEY: It is easier.

MRS. ROONEY: Are you very wet?

MR. ROONEY: To the buff.

MRS. ROONEY: The buff?

MR. ROONEY: The buff. From buffalo.

MRS. ROONEY: We shall hang up all our things in the hot-

38

cupboard and get into our dressing-gowns. (*Pause.*) Put your arm round me. (*Pause.*) Be nice to me! (*Pause. Gratefully.*) Ah, Dan! (*They move on. Wind and rain. Dragging feet, etc. Faintly same music as before. They halt. Music clearer. Silence but for music playing. Music dies.*) All day the same old record. All alone in that great empty house. She must be a very old woman now.

MR. ROONEY: (*indistinctly*). Death and the Maiden.
Silence.

MRS. ROONEY: You are crying. (*Pause.*) Are you crying?

MR. ROONEY: (*violently*). Yes! (*They move on. Wind and rain. Dragging feet, etc. They halt. They move on. Wind and rain. Dragging feet, etc. They halt.*) Who is the preacher tomorrow? The incumbent?

MRS. ROONEY: No.

MR. ROONEY: Thank God for that. Who?

MRS. ROONEY: Hardy.

MR. ROONEY: "How to be Happy though Married"?

MRS. ROONEY: No no, he died, you remember. No connexion.

MR. ROONEY: Has he announced his text?

MRS. ROONEY: "The Lord upholdeth all that fall and raiseth up all those that be bowed down." (*Silence. They join in wild laughter. They move on. Wind and rain. Dragging feet, etc.*) Hold me tighter, Dan! (*Pause.*) Oh yes!
They halt.

MR. ROONEY: I hear something behind us.
Pause.

MRS. ROONEY: It looks like Jerry. (*Pause.*) It is Jerry.
Sound of Jerry's running steps approaching. He halts beside them, panting.

JERRY: (*panting*). You dropped——

39

MRS. ROONEY: Take your time, my little man, you will burst a
blood-vessel.

JERRY: (*panting*). You dropped something, sir. Mr.
Barrell told me to run after you.

MRS. ROONEY: Show. (*She takes the object.*) What is it? (*She
examines it.*) What is this thing, Dan?

MR. ROONEY: Perhaps it is not mine at all.

JERRY: Mr. Barrell said it was, sir.

MRS. ROONEY: It looks like a kind of ball. And yet it is not a ball.

MR. ROONEY: Give it to me.

MRS. ROONEY: (*giving it*). What *is* it, Dan?

MR. ROONEY: It is a thing I carry about with me.

MRS. ROONEY: Yes, but what——

MR. ROONEY: (*violently*). It is a thing I carry about with me!
Silence. Mrs. Rooney looks for a penny.

MRS. ROONEY: I have no small money. Have you?

MR. ROONEY: I have none of any kind.

MRS. ROONEY: We are out of change, Jerry. Remind Mr. Rooney
on Monday and he will give you a penny for your
pains.

JERRY: Yes, Ma'am.

MR. ROONEY: If I am alive.

JERRY: Yessir.
Jerry starts running back towards the station.

MRS. ROONEY: Jerry! (*Jerry halts.*) Did you hear what the hitch
was? (*Pause.*) Did you hear what kept the train so
late?

MR. ROONEY: How would he have heard? Come on.

MRS. ROONEY: What was it, Jerry?

JERRY: It was a——

MR. ROONEY: Leave the boy alone, he knows nothing! Come on!

MRS. ROONEY: What was it, Jerry?

JERRY: It was a little child, Ma'am.
Mr. Rooney groans.

40

MRS. ROONEY: What do you mean, it was a little child?

JERRY: It was a little child fell out of the carriage, Ma'am. (*Pausc.*) On to the line, Ma'am. (*Pause.*) Under the wheels, Ma'am.

Silence. Jerry runs off. His steps die away. Tempest of wind and rain. It abates. They move on. Dragging steps, etc. They halt. Tempest of wind and rain.

END